THE RAVEN DOES NOT RETURN

JEREMIAH KING

THE RAVEN DOES NOT RETURN

CONTENTS

Dedication

I dedicate this book to the Doves in my life...

My God
My Wife
My Boys

I love the family I came from and I am thankful for
the family I created.
God bless you all.

INTRODUCTION

———————

Depression is no place to remain in because Darkness is not your ally. Find the light in your life and run to it, but only if it is sustainable. People change so I do not believe we should make people our anchor. I feel we should search for the unchangeable, and plant our feet firmly in the ground of that soil.

The raven does not return but the dove does ...what is your dove?

DON'T DROWN IN DEPRESSION

GO WITH THE FLOW

I am here for you to cry because crying can lead to being
healed.

I say it is not about me but my actions will appear.
That the world revolves around my sadness and
my cheer.
Show me the rain and I'll show you a smile.
Show me your pain and I'll stay for a while.

Unused potential and deaths are my biggest fears.
Right after that is following the paths of my Peers.

BLINDED

Blinded by Pleasure and you forget the Pain.

Lust corrupts the mind
                    --I guess porn is to blame.

Why avoid the mirror if you haven't any shame?

                    --There's truths in these jokes
                    and *answers* when we entertain.

REST WITH PEACE

———————————

Depression
is the easiest emotion for me to write from
and then Fear; and then Fear of Death.

Joy would be the
hardest.
Yet most needed to be expressed.

So I am hoping that my pain can be the lesson you study
for your own test.
Maybe then God will grant me the peace I seek
as well the mental rest.

FIX ME

_____

Always wanting to be fixed.
                    -but never wanting to do the fixing.

Is like claiming that you're starving but refusing to
cook.
Wanting to know the story but not opening the book.

It's plain to see,
            -well at least to me.
That hero syndrome has you stuck waiting
for a miracle
        --or something spiritual

                            but even that says
                        faith without works is...

HAWKINS

Hawkins, Indiana has to be real.
And   I   must   live   there
Because for every step forward;
I   take   ten   back.
Never   peace   for   long,
Always   chaos   for   longer.

Life full of dark skies and monsters.
I   feel   trapped   upside   down
Never   knowing
what direction I'm supposed to go.

WALKING IN LIMBO

Fork in the road.

I have about six.

My heart has so may passions.

Yet my feet do not move.

I'll never amount to anything

--SO I ask what's the point?

When you'll be forgotten days after you're gone.

So I just stay here.

BOB ROLLING ON A STONE WITH A BEATLE IN NIRVANA

_____

The world is out to get you
Run Run Run
Your parents are trying to mold you
Fun Fun Fun

But I am busy painting pictures of the view
I want to see

Busy yelling at God about who
I am going to be

I once tried to escape but there's no escaping ME
I have made one with the voices
--now you listen when we speak.

STEP IT OUT

BLEEP IT OUT

My dream was not censored
                    -but I'll spare you the details.
              Just know I'll be put away for life
                        if dreams were illegal.

Blood was on my hand, my anger got the best of me.
                    -as I opened my eyes; I felt like
                    it was taking what's left of me.

No analyzing and think pieces,
        because is it ever that deep?
Because you and I know why
I dream like this constantly.

                              Nightmares of Reality

LIVE FROM OCTOBER

———————————

Meet me here, its where my mind resides.
Death is not near. -wipe that look off your face.

    Live from October -Broadcast it to the WORLD!!

If the world is still on the string;
                then start to make it twirl.
Are we all just puppets?
                If so, make us all sing!
I can wave, I can sing, I can do anything.
I am a real boy!

    But I have no control, not even in the world I create
              You rob me of my imagination.
          Now show me what else you can take.

BITE ME

Maybe your bite will *transform* me.
I don't want to be this way any longer.

If you see me as bad.
                    Maybe I should become worse.

Because I feel I have gotten better.

                              But tell me what is that worth?

DARKNESS IS NO ALLY

CRYING WITHOUT TEARS

CRYING WITHOUT TEARS

Lust got me on a schedule
I just want to be free
Algorithms got me shackled
Controlling what I see
Trying to escape but there is no escaping me
Morals keep me from laying with
every girl that I meet
Lines are blurry down here
I forget to pray, is that to real?
Forgive me Lord, I am not my peers
Can you see me crying when there are no tears?

TOUCH THE GRASS

Feet touch the grass
      but blue skies still gray.

I can look you dead in your eyes
      And not hear a word you say.

      Chasing sunsets.
      Make me feel pure
      Just a glimmer of hope
      I know is my cure

AVOID

In these moments I avoid the mirror
Running away from problems like they were never there

Love Me
Love Me

Avoiding all the answers like they're
bad for my health.

Does anyone love me?
Do I love myself?

Chasing peace never chasing wealth
I keep shuffling these cards
Until I like the hand I was dealt.

WHAT IS TRUST?

WHAT IS TRUST?

_____

For just a moment can you show me that it matters if
I am alive.

And God when...
        God, if they do; can you help me believe it.

                        For whats words without actions
        But what has been done without first been spoken.

WOLF

Nothing new under the sun
Well what about the moon
Darkness breeds secrets
And the night can consume
I can wait for the morning
Or I can learn how to howl

DON'T DIE AT THE RED LIGHT

The thing we feel will save us
       is also the thing that will kill us.
So much faith in drawing first
       so little belief in being last.

Praying
for
green
lights.

But until then, we grip
       Grip as tight as we can.

Hoping
to
never
be
caught

in the *red.*

MOVING TO NOT GET LEFT

I do not know how to slow down
Slow represents being stagnant
Being stuck
I need pick me ups
I gotta keep going
The world keeps turning
I feel I am running in place
What can I do to help me catch up?
I am being left behind
Hearts beating fast
I will check it later
I cannot die before I cross the finish line.

I FEEL PRESSURE WHEN YOU ROLL THE WINDOWS UP

That's what she said to me as we left out of the mountains.

It hit me like a ton of bricks.
I pulled over shortly after to look at a horse with the
snow capped mountains behind it.
I quickly wrote what she said down.
She may have been just talking about our ears popping.
But for me it meant so much more.

It meant: you cut my air off and I am suffocating.
I am trapped with nowhere to go.
The walls feel like they are closing in on me.
The pressure is weighing on me.
I need that air.
I need to feel it, smell it, breathe it all in.
I need my windows down.
Don't take my lifeline away.

Help Me Live!

MODUS OPERANDI

I don't stumble in the dark like others.
            You learn how to move in familiar places.

Does it make it right?
Or does it make it wrong

            I will say I am comfortable here.
            But for how much longer.

WHAT IS YOUR
LIGHT?

2009

They thought I left.
> *-I needed that.*

Complete silence.

Alone.
I never felt so alone.

You learn so much about yourself.
When you stop talking.

SOMEWHERE IN FLAGSTAFF

Somewhere in Flagstaff I started thinking.
What am I planting: good or bad?
The constant doubt on what seeds in life I am sowing,
Fruitful seeds that will multiply for good
Or seeds of selfishness that will benefit
no one in the end.

Because you can count the seeds in an apple
but you cannot count the apples in a seed.

To understand that is an honor,

Somewhere in Colorado back to Indiana,
I realized that I am on the right path.

BIG COMFY COUCH

Life was so simple when all I pursued was that couch.
Clowns on a clock;
Sweeping the dust bunnies out.

Now I try to remember that kid;
As I try to make my kids proud.

Ignorance is Bliss

I wish I was still in doubt.

FOX KIDS AND KABOOM

Protection of the young is a beautiful thing.

My favorite cereal we got off of WIC
                              -and I aint know a thing
Fox kids cartoons wasn't on cable
                              -and I aint know a thing
I was a PBS baby reading rainbows
                              I would sing
Library card stacks of books
                              I would read
Personal pan from Pizza Hut
                    was my biggest dream
Rewind the VHS tapes before you return them back

Never forgot how much those who showed you love
                    had your back.

COFFEE BEANS AND CROCKPOTS

Aromas that fills the house,
Usually met with delight.
Can I be that?

Will my presence bring a peace,
Or is my chaos to loud?
Can I be the quiet in your storm?

The coffee in the morning,
The slow cooked meal in the winter.
I want to be;
I desire to be.

N64

We have come so far,
yet we are so far removed.
The more we evolve in the world,

We all can see how much worse we have gotten.
N64 to PS5
Amazing, but at what cost?

I know more about the world than ever before;
but more disconnected from it.
Is there a reset?

Or have we gone too far?

MEN I TRUST

Something in those cords
What is in these melodies
How do you alter my mood when I hit play

From Sade to Men I Trust

I am transported into a calmness I was not in
Is it true that the devil was the angel of music

Power in there
What would the world be without it?
What will the afterlife be with it?

WHICH CAR DO I TAKE?

We all have a destination.
And gifts to help us reach that destination.

Desires can sometimes distract me
from understanding which vehicle best suits me.

Understanding it is not about
how fast I can get there,
but about how effective
the ride can be along the way.

DAY BEFORE MY BIRTHDAY

The day before I celebrate another year of life,
I look back on the year I have had.

And sadly how much closer to death I am.
Am I using my time correctly?

Usually in those reflections I realize I am not.

And then I celebrate;
for I do not know that I will get to celebrate another one.

My heart is always in the right place.
So how can I really be wasting time?

THEY WILL ALWAYS
JUDGE

Nothing you say, do, or create,
can escape criticism?

So

Say, do, and create what your heart desires.

Because they will always judge.
Nothing can stop that.

RUN TO IT

OH, THIS IS YOUR CAR?

Where we are going, the possibilities are endless.
Drive.
Let me map out the steps, tell me where we are headed.
Drive.
How long will we be gone, what time will we be back?
Drive.
How can I drive when I do not know where the car is at...

OCTOBER IS HOME

The whole house is filled with the aroma
when you walk in.
The skies are dark gray;
The wind is blowing.
The rain is falling, the leaves have changed colors;
they lay all over the drive way pavement.
Candles are lit;
the smells of pumpkin and soft musk are mixed in
putting a smile on my face.
The sun has already set.
You can see the porch lights on as you crack the
windows open to let the breeze in.
You walk into the kitchen;
Grab a bowl and fill it up with what has been in the
slow cooker all day.
Head to the table surrounded by love.
Nothing else matters in the moment.
You are simply just thankful,
You are Home.

CHILD'S LAUGH

A child's laugh should make the darkest of hearts beat colors of Joy.

Its the air in the suffocation of day to day interactions with the compromised.

How will we ever return to original thoughts in the corruption.

BROWN COUNTY

I find solitude in a place I have been going to
since a child.
Up the hill,
or down the hill.
I have traveled every corner but the peace is always
brand new,
and greatly welcomed.

Very full and no longer thirsty,
As I head back into the rapture.

SAUNA

I sweat out these toxins;
   hoping to sweat away these sins.
If losing is not an option;
   will me and winning ever mend?

       Standing in a pool of bad choices.
       Wising to do the same to my brain.
       My target is consistency;
       and patience will help me aim.

INK

Sometimes the ink helps you express the words
-you were unable to say.

Rather it's a letter or artwork
Getting it into the world is all that matters.

Like life I have ink I am proud of,
- and a lot I wish I never did.

But the journey of self expression
- is truly the reward.

WATER

Surrounded by
or submerged in
I am a better person
Starting to believe God is water.
Because I feel so pure
When it is near.

MARS HILL

Some of my fondest of memories were created in areas that could be seen as dangerous.
-A black kid
-In the 90s
-In a white neighborhood
-In Indiana

A theme I always follow is the pursuit of child-like innocence.
A time before I understood evil.

My memories were made in that innocence,
And not the corrupted adult mind.
If only everything could stay that way.

OFF THE TOP ROPE

Isn't it strange that everything that brings you
joy as a kid;
                    People shame you for the older you get.
               For still liking or wanting to do those things.

Stop killing peoples joy.

MY SHADOW

I cannot run away from what shows me I am alive.
But I still pretend to not know the truth when you tell
me a lie
1 lie
3 lies
Too many lies
Your body language cannot hide
even in your disguise.

BUT WILL IT LAST?

BETTER MAN

I just want to be a better man

Better man
Better man

Not just for you but for me

Cant you see

Not just for you but for me.

For me
For me

I just want to be free

PORN

It's safer than an affair
                    -but it feels wrong after I finish.

Stimulates my fantasies
                    -and leaves me with guilt.

How much is programmed and how much is DNA?

What's natural for someone with a high sex drive?

Multiple partners doesn't feel right.
But how can one person fulfill all my needs?
Especially when they have needs of their own.
Someone take my hand and lead me to the
                    resolution.

RIGHT WAY

A lot of faiths
A lot of gods
A lot of rules
A lot of directions
A lot of instructors
A lot of words
Even more emotions
No one returns to tell us the right way

So how do we know when we are headed in the
right direction?

RED TAPE

Eyes from hell
I see the evil in your smile

Got the camera on me
All secrets have to die

Death comes with your touch
Skin of a snake

Dry land
I am dying
to make it out of this place.

SWEET TOOTH

I gotta have a taste
Just one and then I will be fine

Until it turns into just once more
Finally every night

Steered so far away from my plan
This map isn't even valid anymore.

OCTOPUS

Swimming to the surface
trying to survive
                        But it has gotten a hold of my leg.

I didn't see it on the surface.
It blended in with everything else.
                I am going to drown if it doesn't let go!

                But as I look down
           I was the only one holding on.

TRAIN

Many destinations

Pick a stop

Second guessing when to exit
is going to leave you in a situation you cannot escape.

How long will you ride,
before it ends your life.

BRICK BY DEFAULT

Stubbornness is an understatement.

I cannot hear a thing when that line is crossed.

Built to last

Brick by brick

Nothing is getting pass me
But I now feel trapped
By not letting you in.

I have built myself into a coffin.
I'll die no longer being able to be hurt by others

Just by my own hand.

APP

I swipe from one to the other
Searching for everything I cannot say
I hate them
But I never leave
And even if I do, I come right back
It's not fear of missing anything
If anything

It's the fear of being *forgotten*.

PAPERMATE

Lightweight
May fly away
Putting my faith in the wrong things
None of it lasts
But yet I search for its replacement.

I never travel far
I still have not found what I am looking for

I love that song
I wonder why...

PEOPLE CHANGE

IS IT ME

_____

Always holding on to a world
    -that feels as if people no longer care is around.

Feeling outnumbered in all my views
The things that bring me joy
    -I am told are wrong by the majority.

I love the cold
Everyone else hates it

I miss video rental stores
Everyone else says "just stream it"

My joy is my Joy
    -but the noise gets heavy

I have searched for like minded people
    -but I always come up empty.

Why am I designed this way?

TIMESHARD

TIMES HAD

I sit back and think about all the time we had;
Times we did not have because they are all in the past.
Funny how tears drop when I remember all the laughs;
It's true time slows down for no one,
its gone way too fast.

I know when I reach your destination it will be my last.

But I hope God is steering my wheel,
because I am not ready to crash.

CONTRADICTIONS

I think we're all contradictions
Of ourselves, losers winning

I think I'm going on and on
I think I'm going about this wrong

I feel we're all contradictions
Of ourselves from the beginning

I think I'll go on alone
I think I'll turn off my phone

I AM NOT THEM

Learn who I am
      So you can discover my intentions
I do not chase fame or clout
I am not desperate to be mentioned

If I support you, I support you
All I need is respect in return

I don't ask questions to steal ideas
I ask questions to learn.

I don't need a handout, I'll get what I earned

I'll make sure to treat people better than you
      when the table turns.

ONE SIDED RELATIONSHIPS

I listen to you
But you don't do the same for me
I ask you questions about your life
You show zero interest in my interests
When I stop calling
The phone doesn't ring
Surrounded by takers
Take, Take, Take
Only so much a giver can give
Before they disappear
But even then, no one would care.

HARM'S WAY

Can you love me
                and put me in bad situations.
Does your own selfishness overcome your judgment
that much?

                                        I may have free will

But my trust for you believes you have the best
intentions for us.
I stand with egg on my face,
I couldn't have been more wrong.

PARENTS

When you have kids of your own you realize how much
your parents did not know.
There really isn't a manual.
There's only teachings, experiences, and lessons
from life and those before us

You realize as you grow, your parents grow

We each experience something we've never experienced
Year to year

Though love still has love attached to it
A little grace goes an eternity

SIDE CHARACTER

We are all the main character in our story
But we all can just play a part in our siblings show
When we were young, we starred together
Now I am lucky to get speaking lines.
There are seasons
Maybe you get brought back at a later time
Maybe you just helped lay the foundation
Wherever the show goes
You are connected forever
Reunions usually happen after the show ends
But in life there are no reruns
Please remember that.

FREE CHOICE

No relation brought us together
You chose me on your own
I appreciate knowing that
Because I have always felt alone
You are not stuck with me by blood
You find joy in being my friend
Tears of joy
All over your shoulder
Loyalty until the end

BEEN HERE

I listen to the elders
Even though this life is nothing like theirs

Their words and experiences are like roots to a tree
Essential to my growth

The moment we disregard those who came before us
Is the moment we lose all that brought us this far

I need the history in this muddy water I am swimming
in
for those lessons help lead me to the spring

FIND AND FLY WITH
YOUR DOVE

WHOLE AGAIN

If you leave
That's part of me
I'll never be whole again.
I could never be whole again

Lacking without your support
Weeping for your touch
Eternity and beyond

Is that asking for too much?

DOMAIN

I search to find what hasn't been taken
What I sometimes believe to be an original thought
                               -I find I come in last place

But instead of quitting with that idea
             I create again

SOIL

Who are we?

Many books describe who we should be

What we should do

But who are we really?
Can the answer of life only be answered in death?

Plant my feet in the soil
Trying not to be moved

For this is the only thing I know to be true

My eyes see it
My skin feels it

It's my soul i don't have an answer to

WING

I hold onto you words
They help me soar

Like I grabbed onto the wing of a dove

Your words are my destination
Where to, never really matters

As long as I am with you

GOD SOUNDS LIKE

How do I explain the feeling I get
when my children laugh

I guess I would say it's what I believe God to sound like
Pure, inescapable joy that fills my entire being
Where nothing in this world matters

What does God sound like to you?

HOME IN YOUR EYES

I hope your eyes are full of love
when they look back at me;

because your eyes are home to me.
I pray God never takes you before me.

Because a picture won't be enough to warm me
from the cold that the absence of your presence brings

RIVER IN THE SNOW

I hear every bird
      every branch
Alone; no matter who's around
The woods in the winter brings forth isolation

Nothing moves fast here
No new technology
You learn so much
If you remain quiet long enough
                  to listen.

NO CRUTCH

I search for help *within*

no pills
no drink
no drugs
no teas
no food

If we're always leaning on something to help us in the
chaos
What happens when it's taken away?

Life is harder without a crutch I will admit

But I want to master this life because
I wont get to do it again

ECHOS

Find me where the noise does not exist.
Where the air is crisp;
Where my voice echos
      through the trees like a herd of deer.
Where the water begins to freeze.
Where the sun shines brighter
      because of the snow.
Look for me and I will be there;
      in silence with a heart full of joy
      and a mind at peace.

STEPS AWAY

All of the answers may not come when you need them.
Sometimes, walking away will provide the clarity.
The push you may need isn't to be done
But to rest.

TOOK THE SKIN OFF

Shed dead weight and drop the mask
Skin came off; free at last!

What's underneath is far more pure.
Something money cannot buy, no one can afford.

Soul made of life decisions
Good or Bad.
There's always forgiveness,
nothing to judge, nothing to see.

Out of the darkness,
and into the light beams.

FILM CAMERAS AND
LILAC FIELDS

Hand me the film camera,
I need something that will last longer than these
phones.
You deserve to run up and down this field.
These colors make your eyes pop even more,
I don't want to say anything.
I just want you to know you how much you are loved;
Your smile.
Those eyes.
That joy.
I wont say a word, I'll just take pictures.
For however long you want to run around;
I'll be running with you.
The image forever in my mind.

I Love You.

THE DOVE RETURNS

You let two go and only one returns.

But yet you spend your days chasing the one that didn't come back.

Let. It. Go.

What you need is right in front of you.
Your eyes may be open, but can you see?

The dove is here.

Never. Let. It. Go.

CONCLUSION

After I wrote my first book *Therapy Had A Waiting List So Here I Am,* I fell right back into depression but I didn't realize it at first. After a couple of weeks of it being released, people started reaching out to sit down and talk about the book. At that point I noticed I was running from it all. I was really proud to have accomplished a goal I had for a long time yet somehow got embarrassed to really talk about the topics or to gain success from the book because I felt like I was still struggling. I self-sabotaged my own success and failed to really have impactful conversations that may have helped not only others but myself as well.

So I started writing this book because the best way for me to express my feelings and thoughts is to write them down. I do not want to get in my own way anymore. I want to defeat depression and I want you too as well. I want to break old habits of disappearing, deleting everything and having to go "get right" before I return. Those days are over!

I had a lot of positive feedback from people on my last book but my mind created a narrative that if this book ever went anywhere people would clown it and say I wasn't a writer. I, honest to God, no longer care what negative comments may come from this book because I really feel good as I type this out right now. I feel I have gotten it all out of my head and onto paper; I am ready to move on and CREATE.

I really hope for those of you reading this who may be struggling with your own depression find something in this book that will help you. People say that all the time but I truly don't want people turning to end their lives, if my words and my own experiences can help in anyway... that's all I really want.

I love and appreciate you!

-Jeremiah

About the Author

Jeremiah King, born and raised in
Indianapolis, Indiana. A husband and a
father to two amazing boys. A creative in
many fields but chooses to express himself
in the current field of the written word.
Currently a second time author of this
series about discovering oneself. Desiring
to leave a legacy of positivity.